SUPER SANDCASTLE
It's the Alphabet!

It's Y!

Oona Gaarder-Juntti

Consulting Editor, Diane Craig, M.A./Reading Specialist

ABDO
Publishing Company

Published by ABDO Publishing Company, 8000 West 78th Street, Edina, Minnesota 55439. Copyright © 2010 by Abdo Consulting Group, Inc. International copyrights reserved in all countries. No part of this book may be reproduced in any form without written permission from the publisher. Super SandCastle™ is a trademark and logo of ABDO Publishing Company.

Printed in the United States.

 PRINTED ON RECYCLED PAPER

Editor: Liz Salzmann
Content Developer: Nancy Tuminelly
Cover and Interior Design and Production: Kelly Doudna, Mighty Media
Photo Credits: iStockphoto (Jani Bryson), Shutterstock

Library of Congress Cataloging-in-Publication Data
Gaarder-Juntti, Oona, 1979-
  It's Y! / Oona Gaarder-Juntti.
      p. cm. -- (It's the alphabet!)
  ISBN 978-1-60453-612-6
  1. English language--Alphabet--Juvenile literature. 2. Alphabet books--Juvenile literature. I. Title.
  PE1155.G2947 2010
  421'.1--dc22
  ⟨E⟩
                              2009022035

Super SandCastle™ books are created by a team of professional educators, reading specialists, and content developers around five essential components—phonemic awareness, phonics, vocabulary, text comprehension, and fluency—to assist young readers as they develop reading skills and strategies and increase their general knowledge. All books are written, reviewed, and leveled for guided reading, early reading intervention, and Accelerated Reader® programs for use in shared, guided, and independent reading and writing activities to support a balanced approach to literacy instruction.

About SUPER SANDCASTLE™

**Bigger Books for Emerging Readers
Grades K–4**

Created for library, classroom, and at-home use, Super SandCastle™ books support and engage young readers as they develop and build literacy skills and will increase their general knowledge about the world around them. Super SandCastle™ books are an extension of SandCastle™, the leading preK–3 imprint for emerging and beginning readers. Super SandCastle™ features a larger trim size for more reading fun.

Let Us Know

Super SandCastle™ would like to hear your stories about reading this book. What was your favorite page? Was there something hard that you needed help with? Share the ups and downs of learning to read. We want to hear from you! Send us an e-mail.

sandcastle@abdopublishing.com

Contact us for a complete list of SandCastle™, Super SandCastle™, and other nonfiction and fiction titles from ABDO Publishing Company.

www.abdopublishing.com • 8000 West 78th Street
Edina, MN 55439 • 800-800-1312 • 952-831-1632 fax

Aa Bb Cc Dd Ee

Ff Gg Hh Ii Jj Kk

Ll Mm Nn Oo Pp

Qq Rr Ss Tt Uu Vv

Ww Xx Yy Zz

The Letter

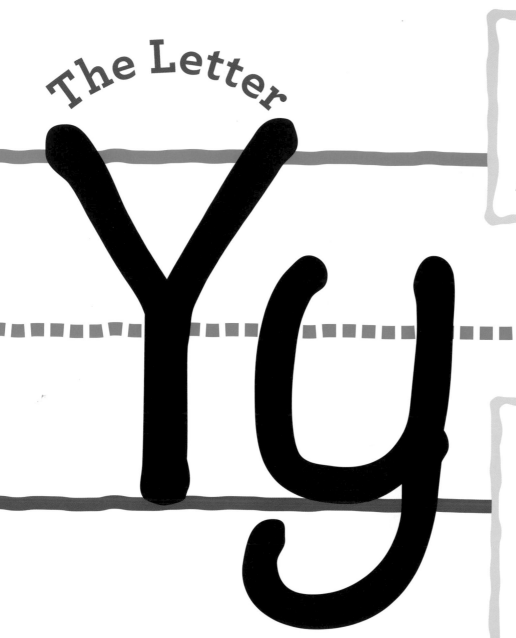

The letter y in
American Sign Language

Y and y
can also look like

Yy **Yy**

Yy Yy

Yy Yy

The letter y
is a consonant.

It is the 25th
letter of the
alphabet.

y as in **y**ellow

yard

yams

yogurt

6

Yuki

Yuki eats yams and yellow yogurt while doing yoga in the yard.

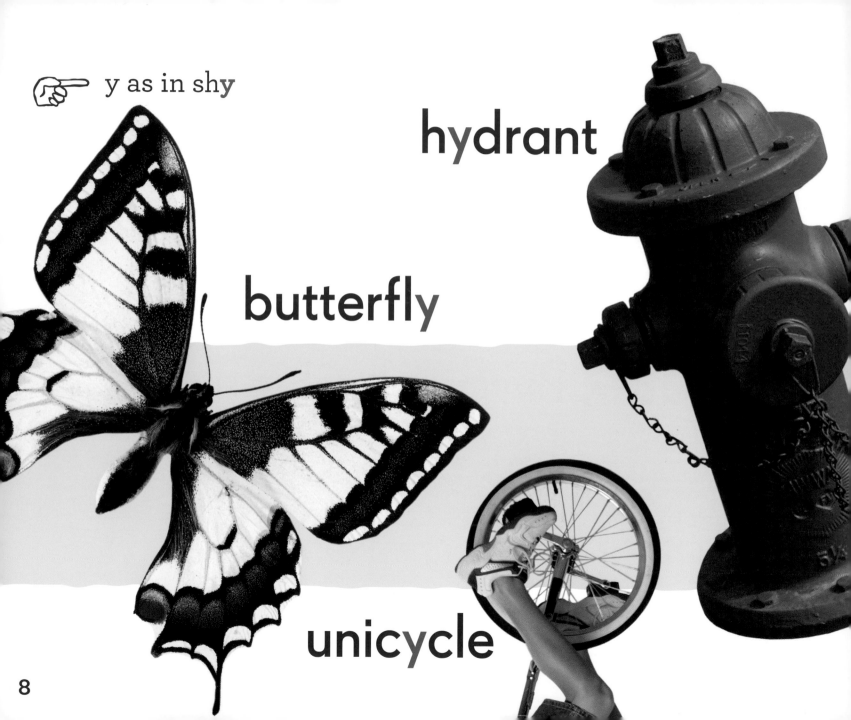

y as in shy

hydrant

butterfly

unicycle

8

Ryan

In July, Ryan rides his unicycle by a shy butterfly on a hydrant.

9

y as in very

bunny

donkey

The letter y is often at the end of a word.

Tony

Tony gets his bunny and donkey ready for a journey to a very lovely valley.

ay as in day

blue jay

hay

crayons

12

Kayla

During the day, Kayla always plays in the hay with her crayons and a blue jay.

Every day Billy the fuzzy yak
sings really loud.

He's not very shy,
and it makes him feel proud.

"We're trying to sleep,"
the monkeys say.

"You don't need to yell,"
cries the blue jay.

But Billy hasn't heard anything for many years.

He has balls of yellow yarn stuck in his ears!

17

"Billy's voice is lovely but loud," says a young butterfly.

"Maybe we can get the yarn out if we really try!"

"I know a very easy way!"
says Sunny the tricky bunny.

"I'll ask Billy into my yard
to eat some yams with honey."

The family of animals gets ready,
hiding behind Sunny's barn.

Then when Billy walks by,
they quickly yank out the yarn!

Which words have the letter **y**?

yams

hamster

butterfly

cap

rock

yarn

monkey

crayon

Glossary

butterfly (pp. 8, 9, 18, 22) – a thin insect with large, brightly colored wings.

fuzzy (p. 15) – covered with hair or fur.

hydrant (pp. 8, 9) – a large outdoor pipe that provides water to put out fires.

journey (p. 11) – a trip or vacation.

really (pp. 15, 18) – very or very much.

stuck (p. 17) – unable to be removed.

unicycle (pp. 8, 9) – a vehicle that has pedals like a bicycle, but has only one wheel and no handlebars.

yak (p. 15) – a large, long-haired ox from Tibet and the mountains of central Asia.

yoga (p. 7) – a system of exercises that involves stretching and staying in certain positions.

yogurt (pp. 6, 7) – a food made with curdled milk and often mixed with fruit.

To promote letter recognition, letters are highlighted instead of glossary words in this series. The page numbers above indicate where the glossary words can be found.

More Words with **Y**

Find the **y** in the beginning, middle, or end of each word.

away	key	toy	yeast	yolk
baby	may	way	yelp	youngster
boy	only	why	yes	your
cry	pony	yawn	yesterday	yourself
eye	sky	yea	yet	youth
fly	today	yeah	yield	yo-yo